EXPLORING THE SCIENCE OF NATURE

The Nature and Science of
NUMBERS

Jane Burton and Kim Taylor

Gareth Stevens Publishing
A WORLD ALMANAC EDUCATION GROUP COMPANY

Please visit our web site at: www.garethstevens.com
For a free color catalog describing Gareth Stevens Publishing's list of high-quality books
and multimedia programs, call 1-800-542-2595 (USA) or 1-800-461-9120 (Canada).
Gareth Stevens Publishing's Fax: (414) 332-3567.

Library of Congress Cataloging-in-Publication Data

Burton, Jane.
The nature and science of numbers / by Jane Burton and Kim Taylor.
p. cm. — (Exploring the science of nature)
Includes bibliographical references and index.
ISBN 0-8368-2193-9 (lib. bdg.)
1. Number concept—Juvenile literature. 2. Science—Juvenile literature.
[1. Number concept. 2. Nature study.] I. Taylor, Kim. II. Title.
QA141.15.B87 2000
513—dc21 00-032248

First published in North America in 2001 by
Gareth Stevens Publishing
A World Almanac Education Group Company
330 West Olive Street, Suite 100
Milwaukee, Wisconsin 53212 USA

Gareth Stevens editors: Barbara J. Behm and Heidi Sjostrom
Cover design: Karen Knutson
Editorial assistant: Diane Laska-Swanke

Printed in the United States of America

1 2 3 4 5 6 7 8 9 05 04 03 02 01

Contents

Words that appear in the glossary are printed in **boldface** type the first time they occur in the text.

How Many?

Numbers play an important role in the natural world. An animal's life is affected by the number of teeth, fingers, toes, or legs it has. A plant is affected by the number of leaves, petals, and seeds it develops.

Some things in the natural world seem countless. The number of pebbles on a beach, raindrops in a thunderstorm, or stars in a **galaxy** are too great to be individually counted. These numbers can only be estimated. For instance, by counting the pebbles on a small part of a beach, the number of pebbles on the entire beach can be estimated.

The number of animals of a particular **species** is vital to their survival. If there are too *few* animals, the species may die out. If there are too *many* animals, they may eat all the available food and then not be able to survive. Some species produce huge numbers of **offspring,** of which only a few survive. Others produce few offspring, of which most survive. The result is that the populations of these particular species remain fairly constant.

Numbers can be applied to time and **inanimate** objects, as well as to living things. Humans use the twenty-four hours of a day and sixty minutes of an hour to keep track of time. The number of days in a **lunar** month and the number of days in a year regulate the lives of many animals.

Above and Opposite: Shell Beach in Western Australia consists of uncountable numbers of pea-sized cockle shells. The shells are piled together by the billions to form the beach, which is over 1/2 mile (1 kilometer) long.

Below: The bodies of starfish are based on the number five.

One Alone

No animals live totally alone because all animals must get together at some point in their lives to **breed**. At other times, many species spend much of their time alone. The big cats in the wild, for example, spend most of their time alone.

The tiger and leopard are solitary creatures. Each member of these species spends much of its time defending its **territory** alone. A lone tiger or leopard knows the importance of holding onto its territory to make sure it has enough food to survive and thrive.

Some birds also defend territories. Male and female European robins each have their own territories during winter, when food is scarce. The ability to defend a territory in winter from any invading robins can make the difference between life and death for the European robin.

In the world of insects, certain types of wasps are known as solitary wasps. Once a female solitary wasp mates, it lives and works entirely alone.

The solitary wasp called the digger wasp digs a **burrow** in hard-packed sand and then hunts for flies. It paralyzes the flies with its sting and then carries them back to the burrow.

The female digger wasp lays her eggs in the flies. The flies become food for the wasp **larvae**. For weeks, the female wasp works alone at these tasks before eventually dying of exhaustion.

Left: A female field digger wasp works entirely on its own. It hunts flies and brings them back to the burrow to feed the wasp larvae.

Two to a Pair

Top: The map butterfly has a pair of antennae and two pairs of wings.

Above: To mate, the male and female large red damselfly join together as a pair.

Many things in the natural world come in twos, or pairs — eyes, legs, and **antennae**, to name just a few. These things often come in pairs because the outside parts of most animals are arranged equally on each side of the middle. Animals have what is known as **bilateral symmetry**, a requirement for walking and crawling. If animals were not symmetrical, they would be lopsided and, therefore, could not move easily and gracefully. For animals that do not move around, symmetry is not quite as important. Body parts on these animals, such as coral, may be arranged in numbers of six or eight.

When animals breed, a pair of them — a male and a female — join together. Most birds form pairs in the breeding season because both parents are needed to **incubate** the eggs and feed the young. These are not the only reasons birds and many other animals breed in pairs, however.

When life first began on Earth, there were no males or females. The offspring produced by living things had the same **genes** as the parent. Offspring were identical to the parents.

This changed after the appearance of males and females on Earth. The pairing of males with females produced offspring with a mixture of genes. The offspring were *not* identical to each other or to either parent. This variety among offspring meant that some individuals were better able to survive changes in the world's climate and to develop quickly into new species.

Multiplying

Top: A male millar's
thumb, or bullhead,
guards a clump of
several hundred
fish eggs.

Top: A male millar's thumb, or bullhead, guards a clump of several hundred fish eggs.

When animals breed, their numbers multiply. Chickens breed quickly and can have several **clutches** of eggs a year. If a pair of chickens raises ten chicks a year and none dies, there will be six times the number of chickens by the end of the year.

What would happen if each female laid a million eggs in a year, as some fish do? The oceans would become choked with fish. Fortunately, only a small percentage of the eggs laid by these fish grows into adults. The rest die off or are eaten long before they grow up. If a female fish lives for five years, she may lay as many as five million eggs. *Just two* of these eggs need to survive into adulthood in order for the population to remain steady.

Right: A female moth may lay over a hundred eggs at one time. Only two of the eggs will need to survive into adulthood to maintain the moth population.

Above: A rooster and a hen might raise ten chicks.

Above: The original population of two chickens multiplies by six to make twelve.

It might seem very wasteful to produce so many eggs, most of which will never grow into adults. However, animal and plant species with the ability to produce huge numbers of offspring are in a good position if conditions in the climate are poor.

If conditions change for the better, there can be disastrous results, however. When rain falls in the desert and plants begin to grow, locusts also multiply quickly. Because each female locust lays several hundred eggs, a **plague** of locusts can be unleashed in a few weeks. The insects sweep over the land, eating everything in their path.

Top: A female rhesus macaque gives birth to only one offspring at a time. The mother looks after the baby very closely.

Below: The paramecium is a single-celled animal that lives in water. Paramecia multiply by splitting in two. They do this every few hours and rapidly increase their numbers.

If, in most cases, it is a positive feature for a species to multiply quickly, why do so many species produce just one or only a few offspring at a time? Some birds lay one egg a year, and many monkeys give birth to a single baby. Because these species take great care of their offspring, they give the young a good chance to survive into adulthood.

The number of eggs a female bird lays depends on the type of bird. The gannet or albatross lives a long life, and the offspring have a good chance of survival. Because of these factors, these birds lay only one egg at a time. The bird called the blue tit has a short life, and many of its offspring die young. This bird lays about ten eggs at a time to make sure some of the young survive.

Single-celled creatures do not lay eggs. They multiply by division. Each single-celled creature splits in half and becomes two creatures.

The two new single-celled creatures divide again to become four. Under favorable conditions, **cell** division can take place every twenty minutes. Therefore, the population of single-celled creatures can double every twenty minutes.

Under just the right conditions, one **bacterium** can become a million bacteria in under seven hours. Such a large mass of bacteria is called a colony. Because bacteria can reach huge numbers in a short time, it is not surprising that diseases spread through a population so quickly.

Above: A blue tit may live for only two or three years, and many of the babies die very young. Adult females must lay around ten eggs at a time to make sure that enough of the offspring survive.

Left: Tasman gannets nest together in large groups on secure rocky islands. Each female lays only one egg at a time. This is enough to maintain the population because gannets live for twenty years or more and many of the young survive to become adults.

Safety in Numbers

Top: A lone red-headed pochard must keep its head up to stay alert to danger.

Many kinds of birds, such as ducks and swans, live together in flocks. Many fish, such as herrings, swim together in schools. Many **mammals**, such as antelopes and zebras, move together in herds. There must be a reason for these animals to gather in such large numbers.

One reason is that many pairs of eyes are better than one at spotting approaching danger. If a single antelope is grazing with its head down, it may not see a **predator** until it is too late. To remain alert to danger, the animal would have to keep raising its head. If it does this too often, it will not get enough to eat. An antelope in a herd

Right: In this mixed flock of mallard and pochard ducks, several birds keep watch for predators. This allows the others to put their heads under the water to feed.

can munch peacefully, raising its head only occasionally. It knows that at least one animal in the herd has its head raised, looking out for danger and standing ready to give the alarm.

There is another reason why animals of one species gather together in large numbers. A predator will find catching one animal in a group more difficult catching an animal that is alone.

A lion will chase a lone zebra until the zebra grows tired and can easily be caught. If there are many zebras, the lion may lose sight of the one it started chasing. It will begin to chase another, and then another, and so on. Eventually, it is the *lion* that grows tired. There is safety in numbers for many types of animals.

Number of Legs

Top: As an insect, the camel cricket has six legs.

The first animals that moved over the Earth many millions of years ago had *no* legs. To move around, they crawled on their bellies over the seabed in which they lived.

Later in time, animals with wormlike bodies gradually developed legs. Their bodies were divided into many segments. The segments had **appendages** on each side that marked the beginnings of legs. The animals moved by wiggling the appendages from side to side.

Today, segmented animals with many legs still exist. The body of a centipede is divided into multiple segments, and every segment has two legs. Millipedes have four legs per segment. Some have as many as five hundred legs in total.

Below: The Mexican superb tarantula is a spider. Spiders have eight legs.

Below: The spiny lobster belongs to the crab family. All crabs have ten legs.

16

Above: The sea slater, a type of woodlouse, has seven segments and a total of fourteen legs.

Above: Centipedes like this one have two pairs of legs per segment. Some have more than one hundred legs.

Too many legs can get in the way of each other. Crabs have reduced their number of legs to ten — and two of these have become **pincers**. Spiders have eight legs, while insects have just six.

Some insects use one of their pairs of legs for special purposes. The hind pair of legs belonging to grasshoppers, crickets, and flea beetles have become very long and strong so that the insects can jump. Water beetles and water boatmen have grown fringes of stiff hairs on their hind legs allowing them to use the legs as "oars." Having six legs allows one pair to be used for special purposes, while the others can still be used for walking.

Below: Millipedes have two pairs of legs per segment. Some have over five hundred legs.

Below: The water boatman's hind legs have developed to become "oars" for swimming.

17

Above: A dog has four legs that are similar to each other. It uses all of them to move around.

Above: The long, strong hind legs of a kangaroo allow it to move quickly. Using all four legs and its tail, it moves slowly.

Below: A mudskipper uses its paired front fins to drag itself over the surface of wet mud.

Animals with backbones, called **vertebrates**, all show the signs of segmented, wormlike ancestors. Their vertebrae and the paired nerves coming from the vertebrae are the remains of segments. Vertebrates usually have either four legs or two legs — unless, of course, they have no legs at all. Most fish have no need for legs, and snakes also manage to crawl around very well without them.

When it comes to the number of legs a land vertebrate has, four is the basic number. These animals all developed from types of fish that crawled around on mud using two pairs of muscular fins. When the first land vertebrates appeared on Earth over 350 million years ago, the pairs of fins had become pairs of legs.

Even today, there are fish called mudskippers that use one pair of fins to crawl and a second pair to cling to rocks and climb trees.

Nearly all mammals have four legs. A few of them, mainly kangaroos, springhares, and jerboas, have developed strong hind legs. This frees their front legs for other purposes, such as holding food. These animals can move quickly by hopping.

Walking on two legs requires good balance, and only birds and humans can walk well. Walking on two hind legs has allowed birds' front legs to develop into wings and humans' front legs to develop hands.

Think of all the examples of this in the natural world. Even some dinosaurs walked on their hind legs and had handlike front legs.

Imagine what humans would now be like if early fish had crawled on three pairs of muscular fins instead of just two pairs. People might now have four hands instead of two!

Above: A silver gull walks on two legs. Over time, its front legs developed into wings.

Left: This dinosaur, Tyrannosaurus rex, thundered along on its massive hind legs. Its front legs became so small that they were almost useless.

19

The Importance of Five

Top: A type of lizard called the gecko has five toes on each foot.

Above: Each flipper of a cape fur seal has five toes enclosed in skin.

Right: The European tree frog has four toes on its front feet and five toes on its hind feet.

Newts, lizards, badgers, and mongooses have five toes on each foot. People also have five toes on each foot, along with five fingers on each hand. There is something special about the number five.

Millions of years ago, fish crawled around on mud with their fins. Each fin contained many tiny bones, called rays. By the time these fish had transformed into four-footed land animals, they had only five rays in each fin. These five-boned fins were the beginning of the pentadactyl limb, which is an arm or leg with five fingers or toes. The legs, arms, or wings of all land vertebrates developed from the pentadactyl limb. *Penta* refers to the number "five," and dactyl refers to "fingers."

Left: A bat's wing is supported by four thin fingers. The thumb projects as a hook half-way along the front edge of the wing.

Below: Cats walk on four toes. The fifth toe on the forefeet is higher up the leg and is used for grasping prey.

Seals and dolphins have five rows of bones in their flippers. Bat wings are supported by four long, thin fingers with a small, projecting thumb.

Cats and dogs have four toes that touch the ground on each paw. On the front legs, however, there may be a fifth toe located a little higher up the leg than the other toes. Often no visible fifth toe can be seen on the hind legs, but there may be a small bone inside the skin. This bone is all that is left of the fifth toe on the hind legs.

Horses walk using just one toe on each foot. Fossils show, however, that today's horses developed from five-toed ancestors.

Sides and Symmetry

Top: This flower is called honesty and belongs to the family Cruciferae. It has four petals that are arranged in the form of a cross.

Radial symmetry occurs when objects are arranged evenly around a central point. Radial symmetry is common in the natural world.

Many flowers are radially symmetrical. Flowers are made up of a ring of petals. Flowers belonging to the same family usually have the same number of petals.

Cabbage flowers and their relatives have four petals arranged equally to form a cross. For this reason, the family is called Cruciferae, from the Latin *crux*, meaning "a cross."

Plant stems are also radially symmetrical. Grasslike plants called sedges have triangular, or three-sided stems. Plants of the Labiatae family, such as mint, have four-sided or square stems.

Right: Large-flower wood sorrel has five symmetrical petals.

Above: Crystals occur when a solid gradually forms from a fluid. Snow crystals take the shape of a six-pointed star.

Above: Amethyst crystals have six sides, reflecting the shape of the silica molecules from which they form.

Five is perhaps the most common number of petals for a flower. Buttercup, campion, primrose, rose, and apple flowers all have five equal petals. Flowers with six petals are also common.

Crystals of snow occur in various hexagonal, or six-sided, forms. The exact arrangement depends on temperatures in the atmosphere when the crystals form. Quartz crystals also have six sides. The crystals build up in layers, each one **molecule** thick.

Regular hexagons fit together neatly in rows. Wasps and bees build their honeycombs of six-sided wax cells.

Left: A paper wasp's nest in Australia is built of six-sided cells.

This bristlecone pine tree in California was probably about four thousand years old when it died. The oldest known tree was 4,900 years old when it was cut down.

Count the Years

Top: Each ridge on a flat oyster shell marks a year's growth. This shell was six years old when the animal inside of it died.

One year is 365 days long. That is the length of time in which Earth travels once around the Sun. The seasons that take place during each year are very important to the natural world.

Winters in **temperate** and **polar** regions are cold enough to make plants stop growing. Many animals are affected, too. Fish sink to the bottom of lakes. Snakes and lizards creep into holes in the ground or cracks in rocks, where they lie motionless during the cold months.

When the growth of trees and other woody plants slows down in autumn, cells in the outer layer of wood become smaller and more tightly packed. Rapid growth in spring and summer produces bigger cells, and consequently softer wood. Alternating layers of hard and soft wood produces the grain in wood. These layers become clearly visible if the trunk of a tree is sawn across to reveal its **annual rings**. A tree's age, in years, is determined by counting the rings. The thickness of each ring shows how well the tree grew in any particular year.

The scales of some fish also have annual rings. Fish do not shed their skins like snakes. Instead, their scales grow a little each year. The number of rings on a fish's scales reveals the fish's age in years.

Above: Annual growth rings are clearly visible in this slice of a Douglas fir tree.

Below: The scales on the flank of this golden carp show faint growth rings. In order that the rings be counted, a scale must be examined under a microscope.

25

Billions

How many grains of sand exist on a beach? How many leaves grow in a forest? How many stars shine in the sky? Billions and billions!

A billion is one thousand million. Over six billion people live in the world. Probably no other species of mammal, bird, or reptile is as numerous as humans. The most common mammal, bird, or reptile species can be counted in the millions, not billions. In the animal world, only insects can be counted in the billions.

The smallest living creatures, such as **protozoa** and bacteria, multiply so quickly and occupy so little space that as many as a billion can be found in a bucketful of water from a stagnant pond.

Above: When an acorn falls on **fungi** called puffballs, billions of spores are released into the air. Each spore is capable of growing into another puffball, but only a few of them do.

Right: Millions of spire shell creatures crawl over the mud at low tide on this Gambia River beach in West Africa.

Left: There are billions of stars in our galaxy and billions of galaxies in the universe. This small section of the night sky shows the constellation called the Great Bear, or the Big Dipper.

Molecules are so amazingly small that a tiny drop of water contains billions and billions of them.

A single galaxy can contain billions of stars, and there are billions of galaxies in the universe. With this vast number of stars — each of which is like our Sun — it is quite possible that some type of life exists in other parts of the universe.

The natural world isn't the only place that concerns itself with numbers. The daily lives of human beings are filled with numbers. People count time in years, months, days, minutes, and seconds. They know how many miles (kilometers) and the amount of time it takes to get from place to place. Children know how old they are and what grade they are in. They know their address and telephone number.

People count money, sheep, sports scores, and many, many other things. The amount of time we spend thinking of numbers in our lives is countless.

Below: Millions of gorse spider mites will sometimes spin their webs in gorse bushes, giving the bushes a silvery sheen.

Activities:

Can You Count?

Counting is not always the way to answer the question, "How many?" For instance, the number of birds in a large flock often cannot be counted because the birds keep moving, and the flock may be visible for only a short time. In situations such as this, the number can only be estimated.

Good Judgment

Estimating numbers requires good judgment and a lot of practice. The quick way to estimate the number of birds in a large flock is to count about ten or twenty birds that are flying close together. Then, make a mental note of the area that they occupy.

Next, mentally divide the flock into ten-bird (or twenty-bird) areas, and count the number of these areas. If the flock consists of nine ten-bird areas, the estimated total is ninety. If the flock consists of four twenty-bird areas, the estimated total is eighty.

Counting Daisies

When the objects that need counting are not moving, but yet are too numerous to count individually, another method can be used. An estimate can be made using a system of quadrats. A quadrat is a square area used in population studies, especially studies of plant populations.

To count the number of daisies growing in a field (*left*), you will need some stiff wire and a pair of wire cutters strong enough to cut and bend the wire. You will also need tape, a tape measure, a notebook, a pen or pencil, and a calculator (*above*).

Bend the wire at right angles four times to form a square with precisely half-foot or half-meter sides. Tape the ends together.

With your square, notebook, and pen or pencil in hand, walk diagonally across the field, dropping the square every few steps. Alternate the side on which you drop it — first on your left, then on your right. Close your eyes before choosing each spot. Otherwise, you might be tempted to select areas that have the most daisies. The idea is to choose the quadrats at random.

Drop the square as many times as you want. Each time you drop the square, count and write down the number of daisies the square contains. If there are no daisies in the square, be sure to record a zero.

Using the calculator, add the total number of daisies you counted in all of the squares. Then divide this by the number of quadrats. This gives you the average number of daisies per quadrat. Multiply this figure by four, and you have the average number of daisies per square foot or meter.

Next, measure the field and figure out its total area in square feet or meters. Multiply

this figure by the average number of daisies per square foot or square meter. This final figure is an estimate of the total number of daisies growing in the field.

Simple Multiplication

Watch the progress of multiplication in the natural world by observing the plant called duckweed. Duckweed has small, green leaves that float on the surface of water. It multiplies by budding.

Each leaf produces little leaves that break off and grow before they themselves start budding. This is not the same way that bacteria multiply, but the effect is similar, just slower.

To do this experiment, place a bowl of water on a windowsill that gets plenty of light. Place one healthy leaf of duckweed in the bowl, and wait to see it multiply.

Each day, count the number of leaves (*left*). Events will happen slowly at first, but suddenly, you will find there are almost too many leaves to count. Numbers can quickly build up even when there is a fairly slow rate of multiplication.

Counting Toes

Next time you visit a zoo, see how many toes each kind of animal has. You should be able to find animals with one toe per foot (horses), two toes (cows), three toes (guinea pigs), four toes (cats), and five toes (lizards).

Below: Occasionally, kittens are born with more toes than normal. This kitten has six toes on each foot!

29

Glossary

annual rings: rings that can be seen in structures such as wood and fish scales that show seasonal changes in growth rates.

antennae: the pair of feelers on the head of an insect.

appendages: the small extensions attached to the body of an animal.

bacterium: a microscopic creature found almost everywhere on Earth. *Bacteria* is the plural.

bilateral symmetry: the quality of having two sides that are mirror images of each other.

breed (v): to join together for the purpose of producing young.

burrow: a hole an animal makes in the ground for use as shelter and habitat.

clutches: nests or groups of eggs.

fungi: spore-producing organisms, such as molds, mildews, mushrooms, and yeasts. *Fungus* is the singular.

galaxy: a collection of vast numbers of stars.

genes: the material in a cell that determines the characteristics that are passed on from parent to child. There are thousands of genes in a cell, and each cell in an animal or plant contains the same set of genes.

inanimate: not living or not able to move.

incubate: to keep warm.

larvae: the earliest stages in the growth of insects.

lunar: relating to the Moon.

mammals: warm-blooded, furry animals that nourish their young with the mother's milk.

mate (v): to unite or join together with another member of the same species for the purpose of producing offspring.

molecule: the smallest part of a substance, made up of two or more atoms joined together.

offspring: young plants or animals produced by a set of parents.

pincers: claws used for gripping objects.

plague: a large, destructive invasion.

polar: referring to areas around the ends of Earth's axis.

predator: an animal that hunts other animals for food.

protozoa: the name for animals that consist of a single cell.

radial symmetry: arranged evenly in a circular fashion.

species: a biologically distinct kind of animal or plant. Similar species are grouped into the same genus.

temperate: referring to areas of Earth where the climate is without extremes.

territory: the area of land that an animal (or group of animals) occupies and defends.

Plants and Animals

The common names of plants and animals vary from language to language. Their scientific names, based on Greek or Latin words, are the same the world over. Each kind of plant or animal has two scientific names. The first name is called the genus. It starts with a capital letter. The second name is the species name. It starts with a small letter.

blood-red starfish (*Henricia sanguinolenta*) — Caribbean 5

bristlecone pine (*Pinus aristata*) — North America 24

cape fur seal (*Arctocephalus pusillus*) — coasts of southern Africa 20

Douglas fir (*Pseudotsuga menziesii*) — North America, grown worldwide 25

European robin (*Erithacus rubecula*) — Europe 6

European tree frog (*Hyla arborea*) — Europe 20

field digger wasp (*Mellinus arvensis*) — Europe 7

flat oyster (*Ostrea edulis*) — North Atlantic 25

impala (*Aepyceros melampus*) — Africa 15

kongoni or coke's hartebeest (*Alcelaphus cokei*) — Africa 15

large red damselfly (*Pyrrhosoma nymphula*) — Europe 8

large-flower wood sorrel (*Oxalis purpurea*) — South Africa 22

mallard (*Anas platyrhynchos*) — North America, Europe, Asia 14

mudskipper (*Periophthalmus barbarus*) — Australia, Africa, India, South Pacific 18

mute swan (*Cygnus olor*) — Europe 9

puffball (*Lycoperdon species*) — Europe 26

rhesus macaque (*Macaca mulatta*) — India, Southeast Asia 12

sea slater (*Ligia oceanica*) — North Atlantic shores 17

silver gull (*Larus novaehollandiae*) — Australia 19

superb tarantula (*Euanthlus bohemi*) — Mexico 16

Tasman gannet (*Morus serrator*) — coasts of Australia and New Zealand 7, 13

tiger (*Panthera tigris*) — Asia 6

water boatman (*Notonecta glauca*) — Europe 17

Books to Read

Centipedes. The New Creepy Crawly Collection (series). Graham Coleman (Gareth Stevens)

How Animals Protect Themselves. Animal Survival (series). Michel Barré (Gareth Stevens)

In Peril (series). Barbara J. Behm and Jean-Christophe Balouet (Gareth Stevens)

Insects. Young Scientist Concepts & Projects (series). Jen Green (Gareth Stevens)

Spotlight on Spiders. Nature Close-Ups (series). Densey Clyne (Gareth Stevens)

Wild Cats. Welcome to the World of Animals (series). Diane Swanson (Gareth Stevens)

Videos and Web Sites

Videos

Animals of Africa: Big Cats of the Kalahari. (Just For Kids Home Video)
Audubon Society's Video Guide: Birds of North America 5. (Mastervision)
Flowers, Plants, and Trees. (Library Video)
Insects. (TMW Media)
Insects: The Little Things That Run the World. (Unapix)

Web Sites

www.doscience.com
www.planetpets.simplenet.com/plntamba.htm
www.utm.edu/`rirwin/symmetry2.htm
www.bergen.org/AAST/Projects/ES/AP/Index2.html
www.greatcatsoftheworld.com/
www.earthlife.net/insects/six.html

Some web sites stay current longer than others. For further web sites, use your search engines to locate the following topics: *bilateral symmetry, centipedes, endangered animals,* and *protozoa.*

Index